BEGINNER'S KANA WORKBOOK

Practice Drills for Writing Hiragana and Katakana

Fujhiko Kaneda

Calligraphy by Masaya Katayama

PASSPORT BOOKS
NTC/Contemporary Publishing Group

About the Authors
Fujihiko Kaneda, a graduate of Osaka University of Foreign Studies, is extremely interested in studying new methods of teaching Japanese to both serious foreign students and people who are interested in the Japanese language.
Other books:
Yohan English-Japanese, Japanese-English Dictionary
Easy Hiragana
Easy Kanji
Fuji-Tokaido

Masaya Katayama, born in Osaka, has produced many books as an editor, proofreader and translator. In addition to those pursuits he is also a student of practical calligraphy. He has cooperated as a calligrapher for the production of all of the Japanese writing books of Fujihiko Kaneda. Readers will also enjoy his sample letters in this book, and students can master the writing of *hiragana* and *katakana* in a short period of time.

Cover design by Takashi Suzuki
Interior illustrations by Kazuo Ishizuka
Pen calligraphy by Masaya Katayama

Published by Passport Books
A division of NTC/Contemporary Publishing Group, Inc.
4255 West Touhy Avenue, Lincolnwood (Chicago), Illinois 60712-1975 U.S.A.
Copyright © 1996 by Yohan Publications, Inc.
Printed in the United States of America
International Standard Book Number: 0-8442-8373-8

3 4 5 6 7 8 9 0 VLP VLP 0 5 4 3 2 1

DO-IT-YOURSELF KANA CHARTS

Fill in the following charts, writing *hiragana* in the left part of each box and *katakana* in the right. Then check your entries against the charts in the "Explanation of *Kana*" on pages 9–11.

Basic Kana Symbols

VOWELS

	a	i	u	e	o
	a	i	u	e	o
k	ka	ki	ku	ke	ko
s	sa	shi	su	se	so
t	ta	chi	tsu	te	to
n	na	ni	nu	ne	no
h	ha	hi	fu	he	ho
m	ma	mi	mu	me	mo
y	ya		yu		yo
r	ra	ri	ru	re	ro
w	wa				wo
n	n				

CONSONANTS

Basic Voiced Sounds

	a	i	u	e	o
g	ga	gi	gu	ge	go
z/j	za	ji	zu	ze	zo
d/z/j	da	ji	zu	de	do
b	ba	bi	bu	be	bo
p	pa	pi	pu	pe	po

Basic Combinations

	a	u	o
ky	kya	kyu	kyo
sh	sha	shu	sho
ch	cha	chu	cho
ny	nya	nyu	nyo
hy	hya	hyu	hyo
my	mya	myu	myo
ry	rya	ryu	ryo

Voiced Combinations

	a	u	o
gy	gya	gyu	gyo
j	ja	ju	jo
j	ja	ju	jo
by	bya	byu	byo
py	pya	pyu	pyo

Final Review

DO-IT-YOURSELF KANA CHARTS

Fill in the following charts, writing *hiragana* in the left part of each box and *katakana* in the right. Then check your entries against the charts in the "Explanation of *Kana*" on pages 9–11.

Basic Kana Symbols

VOWELS

	a	*i*	*u*	*e*	*o*
	a	*i*	*u*	*e*	*o*
k	*ka*	*ki*	*ku*	*ke*	*ko*
s	*sa*	*shi*	*su*	*se*	*so*
t	*ta*	*chi*	*tsu*	*te*	*to*
n	*na*	*ni*	*nu*	*ne*	*no*
h	*ha*	*hi*	*fu*	*he*	*ho*
m	*ma*	*mi*	*mu*	*me*	*mo*
y	*ya*		*yu*		*yo*
r	*ra*	*ri*	*ru*	*re*	*ro*
w	*wa*				*wo*
n	*n*				

CONSONANTS

Basic Voiced Sounds

	a	i	u	e	o
g	ga	gi	gu	ge	go
z/j	za	ji	zu	ze	zo
d/z/j	da	ji	zu	de	do
b	ba	bi	bu	be	bo
p	pa	pi	pu	pe	po

Basic Combinations

	a	u	o
ky	kya	kyu	kyo
sh	sha	shu	sho
ch	cha	chu	cho
ny	nya	nyu	nyo
hy	hya	hyu	hyo
my	mya	myu	myo
ry	rya	ryu	ryo

Voiced Combinations

	a	u	o
gy	gya	gyu	gyo
j	ja	ju	jo
j	ja	ju	jo
by	bya	byu	byo
py	pya	pyu	pyo

JAPANESE PLACE NAMES QUIZ

Fill the blanks with the correct *kana* from the list on the facing page.

Cities

1. Tokyo   _____
2. Sapporo   _____
3. Sendai   _____
4. Yokohama   _____
5. Nagoya   _____
6. Osaka   _____
7. Hiroshima   _____
8. Kyoto   _____
9. Nagasaki   _____
10. Kobe   _____
11. Fukuoka   _____

Islands and prefectures

1. Honshu   _____
2. Chiba Prefecture   _____
3. Kyushu   _____
4. Hokkaido   _____
5. Gifu Prefecture   _____
6. Shikoku   _____
7. Saitama Prefecture   _____
8. Hyogo Prefecture   _____
9. Kumamoto Prefecture   _____
10. Kanagawa Prefecture   _____
11. Okinawa   _____

Contents

Author's Preface

In 1995, we published EASY KANJI, the third book in the Easy Japanese Writing triology after EASY KATAKANA and EASY HIRAGANA. This EASY HIRAGANA/KATAKANA WORKBOOK is written for beginners who want to write Japanese and who wish to learn to write the language in a shorter period of the time the above title would require.

We have simplified the explanations of basic steps in writing Japanese and increased the practical exercise pages. With this workbook, readers can study to write not only words but also longer sentences.

Students will learn hiragana writing in the first chapter, and katakana in the second. In the third chapter they can study many sentences constructed with both hiragana and katakana.

Considering the number of children learning Japanese is increasing now in the world, we have included various illustrations in the text to make the study of written Japanese more pleasurable, to encourage readers to study the work through to the end.

I hope this book is useful for all learners of the Japanese language.

Fujihiko Kaneda

The Basics of Written Hiragana

The general stroke order in writing *hiragana*

1.   Write a horizontal stroke from left to right.
2.   Write a vertical line from top to bottom.

Three ways to end a stroke

1.   *Tome* (Stop)

  Stop the pen or pencil completely by pressing it against the paper slightly.

mae	*inu*	*neko*
(front)	(dog)	(cat)

2.   *Hane* (Jump)

  End the stroke with a small reflex tail in another direction.

kasa	*take*	*hari*
(umbrella)	(bamboo)	(needle)

3.   *Harai* (Sweep)

  Write this stroke by lifting the pen or pencil, gradually moving the hand to the end of the stroke.

ushi	*tsume*	*asu*
(cattle)	(fingernail)	(tomorrow)

HIRAGANA

Basic Hiragana (46)

あ	い	う	え	お
a	i	u	e	o
か	き	く	け	こ
ka	ki	ku	ke	ko
さ	し	す	せ	そ
sa	shi	su	se	so
た	ち	つ	て	と
ta	chi	tsu	te	to
な	に	ぬ	ね	の
na	ni	nu	ne	no

は
ha

ひ
hi

ふ
fu

へ
he

ほ
ho

ま
ma

み
mi

む
mu

め
me

も
mo

や
ya

ゆ
yu

よ
yo

ら
ra

り
ri

る
ru

れ
re

ろ
ro

わ
wa

を
o

ん
n/m

Dakuon (20) and Handakuon (5)

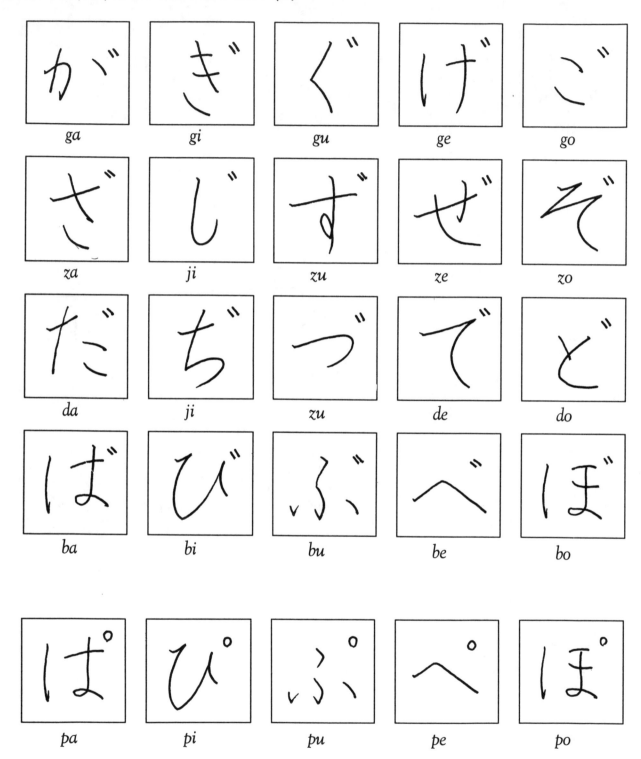

が	ぎ	ぐ	げ	ご
ga	gi	gu	ge	go
ざ	じ	ず	ぜ	ぞ
za	ji	zu	ze	zo
だ	ぢ	づ	で	ど
da	ji	zu	de	do
ば	び	ぶ	べ	ぼ
ba	bi	bu	be	bo
ぱ	ぴ	ぷ	ぺ	ぽ
pa	pi	pu	pe	po

Basic Yōon (21)

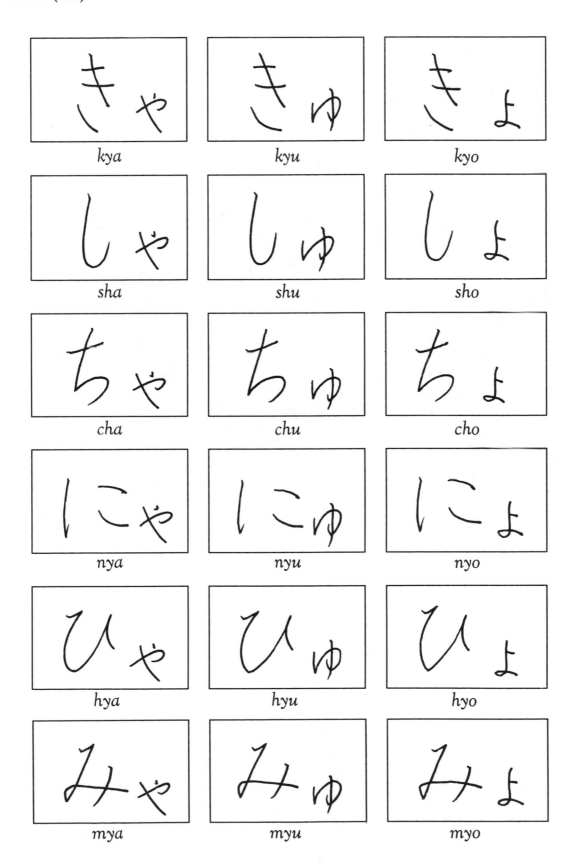

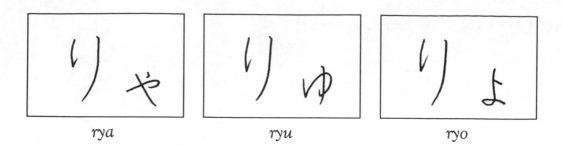

rya	*ryu*	*ryo*

Voiced (12)/Semi-voiced (3) Yōon

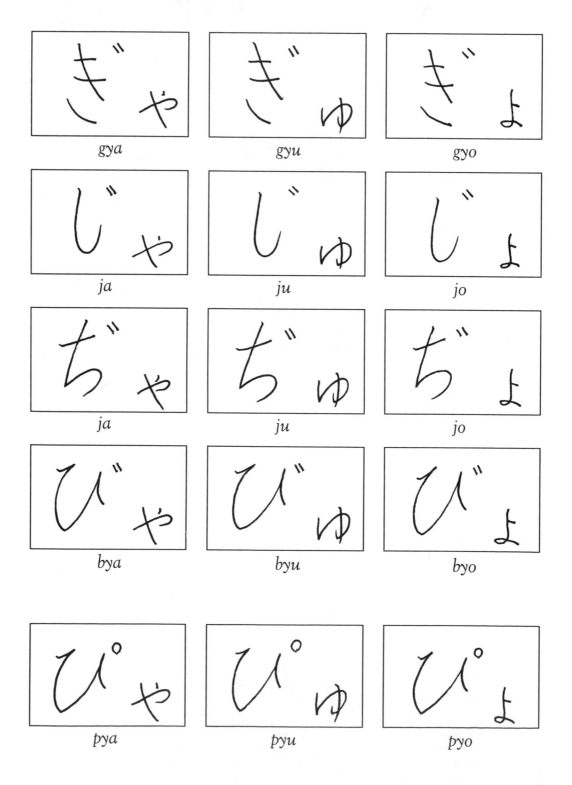

gya	*gyu*	*gyo*
ja	*ju*	*jo*
ja	*ju*	*jo*
bya	*byu*	*byo*
pya	*pyu*	*pyo*

How to Write Hiragana

For practice, trace over the dotted lines and complete each example.

ku						

shi						

he						

i						

11

ko						

ki						

ma						

mo						

tsu	つ	つ				
	つ	つ	つ	つ	つ	つ
no	の	の	の	の	の	の
	の	の	の	の	の	の
wa	わ	わ	わ	わ	わ	わ
	わ	わ	わ	わ	わ	わ
yu	ゆ	ゆ	ゆ	ゆ	ゆ	
	ゆ	ゆ	ゆ	ゆ	ゆ	ゆ

su	す	→	ず	す	す	す
	す	す	す	す	す	す

se	せ	→	サ	せ	せ	せ
	せ	せ	せ	せ	せ	せ

te	て	て	て	て	て	て
	て	て	て	て	て	て

so	そ	そ	そ	そ	そ	そ
	そ	そ	そ	そ	そ	そ

ni	に	↓し	にﾞ	に	に	に
	に	に	に	に	に	に

ke	け	↓し	にﾞ	け		
	け	け	け	け	け	け

ha	は	↓し	にﾞ	ば	は	は
	は	は	は	は	は	は

ho	ほ	↓し	にﾞ	にﾞ	ぼ	ほ
	ほ	ほ	ほ	ほ	ほ	ほ

ka	か	ゔ	か	が		
	か	か	か	か	か	か

hi	ひ	ひ				
	ひ	ひ	ひ	ひ	ひ	ひ

fu	ふ	゛	ふ	ふ	ふ	
	ふ	ふ	ふ	ふ	ふ	ふ

mi	み	み	み			
	み	み	み	み	み	み

chi	ち	ー	ち			
	ち	ち	ち	ち	ち	ち

o	お	ー	お	お		
	お	お	お	お	お	お

a	あ	ー	さ	あ		
	あ	あ	あ	あ	あ	あ

ya	や	つ	づ	や		
	や	や	や	や	や	や

sa	さ	→	ヤ	さ		
	さ	さ	さ	さ	さ	さ

ta	た	→	ヂ	た	た	
	た	た	た	た	た	た

na	な	→	ヤ	な	な	
	な	な	な	な	な	な

o	を	→	青	を		
	を	を	を	を	を	を

ro	ろ	ろ				
	ろ	ろ	ろ	ろ	ろ	ろ
ru	る	る				
	る	る	る	る	る	る
me	め	め	め			
	め	め	め	め	め	め
nu	ぬ	ぬ	ぬ			
	ぬ	ぬ	ぬ	ぬ	ぬ	ぬ

u	う	↙	う			
	う	う	う	う	う	う

ri	り	↓	り			
	り	り	り	り	り	り

yo	よ	↙	よ			
	よ	よ	よ	よ	よ	よ

to	と	↓	と			
	と	と	と	と	と	と

ra	ら	ら	ら			
	ら	ら	ら	ら	ら	ら
re	れ	れ	れ			
	れ	れ	れ	れ	れ	れ
ne	ね	ね	ね			
	ね	ね	ね	ね	ね	ね
e	え	え	え			
	え	え	え	え	え	え

mu	む	ー	む	む		
	む	む	む	む	む	む

n	ん	ん				
	ん	ん	ん	ん	ん	ん

The Basics of Written Katakana

The general stroke order in writing *katakana* is exactly same as in *hiragana.*

1. Write a horizontal stroke from left to right.
2. Write a vertical line from top to bottom.

Three ways to end a stroke

1. *Tome* (Stop)

    Stop the pen or pencil completely by pressing it against the paper slightly.

ki	*mo*	*mi*

2. *Hane* (Jump)

    End the stroke with a small reflex tail in another direction.

ka	*ho*	*o*

3. *Harai* (Sweep)

    Write this stroke by lifting the pen or pencil, gradually moving the hand to the end of the stroke.

tsu	*ra*	*shi*

The strokes of *katakana* are written with acute angles and rectangular figures. They are in marked contrast to *hiragana* written with curved lines. Note this point when you write *katakana.*

KATAKANA

Basic Katakana (46)

ア	イ	ウ	エ	オ
a	*i*	*u*	*e*	*o*
カ	キ	ク	ケ	コ
ka	*ki*	*ku*	*ke*	*ko*
サ	シ	ス	セ	ソ
sa	*shi*	*su*	*se*	*so*
タ	チ	ツ	テ	ト
ta	*chi*	*tsu*	*te*	*to*
ナ	ニ	ヌ	ネ	ノ
na	*ni*	*nu*	*ne*	*no*

ha hi fu he ho

ma mi mu me mo

ya   yu   yo

ra ri ru re ro

wa   o

n/m

Dakuon (20) and Handakuon (5)

ガ	ギ	グ	ゲ	ゴ
ga	*gi*	*gu*	*ge*	*go*
ザ	ジ	ズ	ゼ	ゾ
za	*ji*	*zu*	*ze*	*zo*
ダ	ヂ	ヅ	デ	ド
da	*ji*	*zu*	*de*	*do*
バ	ビ	ブ	ベ	ボ
ba	*bi*	*bu*	*be*	*bo*
パ	ピ	プ	ペ	ポ
pa	*pi*	*pu*	*pe*	*po*

Yōon (36)

Basic Yōon (21)

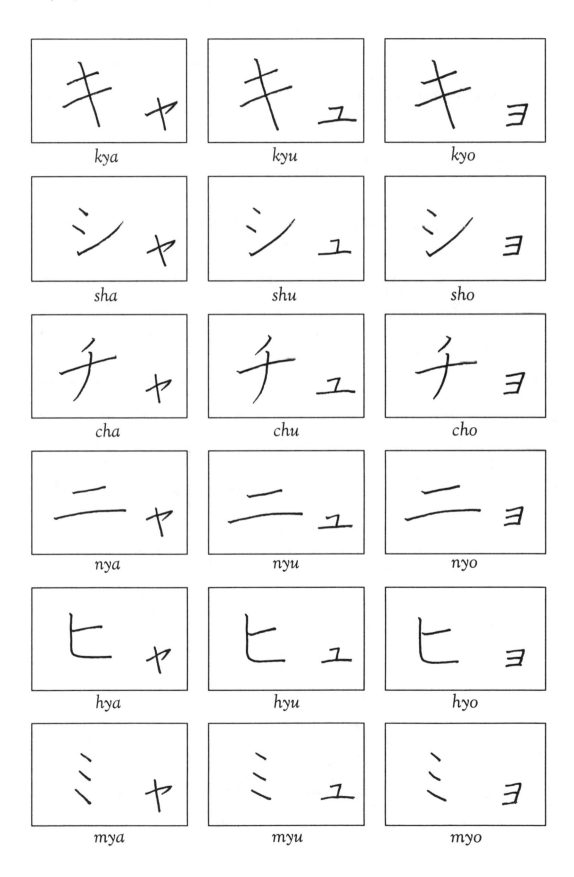

キャ	キュ	キョ
kya	kyu	kyo
シャ	シュ	ショ
sha	shu	sho
チャ	チュ	チョ
cha	chu	cho
ニャ	ニュ	ニョ
nya	nyu	nyo
ヒャ	ヒュ	ヒョ
hya	hyu	hyo
ミャ	ミュ	ミョ
mya	myu	myo

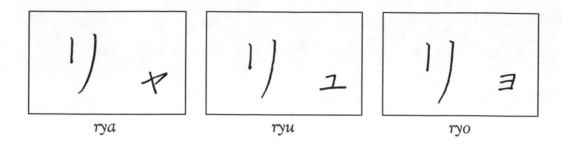

rya   ryu   ryo

Voiced (12)/Semi-voiced (3) Yōon

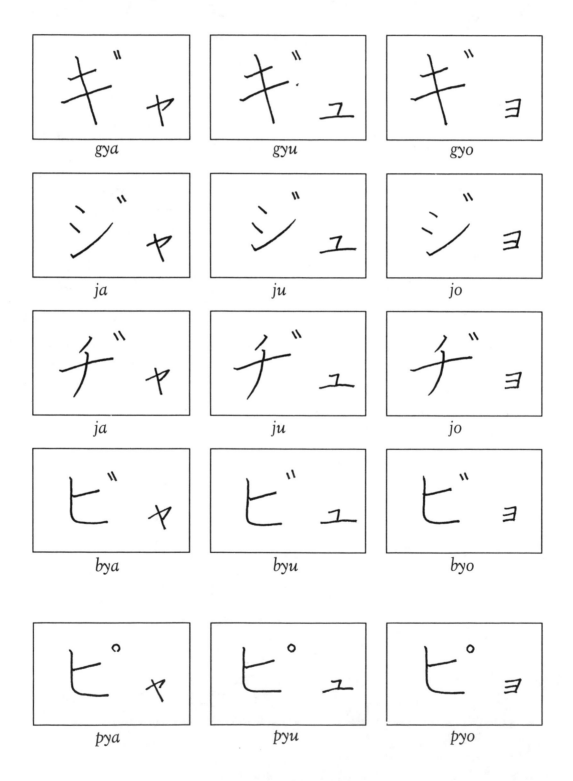

gya   gyu   gyo

ja   ju   jo

ja   ju   jo

bya   byu   byo

pya   pyu   pyo

How to Write *Katakana*

For practice, trace over the dotted lines and complete each example.

no	ノ	ノ				
	ノ	ノ	ノ	ノ	ノ	ノ
i	イ	イ	イ			
	イ	イ	イ	イ	イ	イ
so	ソ	ソ	ソ			
	ソ	ソ	ソ	ソ	ソ	ソ
tsu	ツ	ツ	ツ	ツ		
	ツ	ツ	ツ	ツ	ツ	ツ

na	ナ	→	ナ			
	ナ	ナ	ナ	ナ	ナ	ナ

ni	二	→	二			
	二	二	二	二	二	二

te	テ	→	二	テ		
	テ	テ	テ	テ	テ	テ

chi	チ	↙	ン	チ		
	チ	チ	チ	チ	チ	チ

ku	ク	⸍	ク			
	ク	ク	ク	ク	ク	ク
ta	タ	⸍	ク	タ		
	タ	タ	タ	タ	タ	タ
mu	ム	⼚	ム			
	ム	ム	ム	ム	ム	ム
a	ア	⼆	ア			
	ア	ア	ア	ア	ア	ア

ha	ノ ハ	↙リ	ノ ハ↘			
	ハ	ハ	ハ	ハ	ハ	ハ

he	ヘ	↗ヘ↘				
	ヘ	ヘ	ヘ	ヘ	ヘ	ヘ

ri	リ	↓丨	リ↓			
	リ	リ	リ	リ	リ	リ

mi	ミ	↗	↗	↗		
	ミ	ミ	ミ	ミ	ミ	ミ

wa	ワ	い	ワ			
	ワ	ワ	ワ	ワ	ワ	ワ
ra	ラ	→	ラ			
	ラ	ラ	ラ	ラ	ラ	ラ
ma	マ	マ	マ			
	マ	マ	マ	マ	マ	マ
u	ウ	↓	い	ウ		
	ウ	ウ	ウ	ウ	ウ	ウ

fu	フ	フ				
	フ	フ	フ	フ	フ	フ
yu	ユ	フ	ユ			
	ユ	ユ	ユ	ユ	ユ	ユ
ko	コ	フ	コ			
	コ	コ	コ	コ	コ	コ
yo	ヨ	フ	ヨ	ヨ		
	ヨ	ヨ	ヨ	ヨ	ヨ	ヨ

me	メ	⅃	⅄			
	メ	メ	メ	メ	メ	メ

ka	カ	⅂	カ			
	カ	カ	カ	カ	カ	カ

sa	サ	一	⅄	サ		
	サ	サ	サ	サ	サ	サ

ke	ケ	⅃	一	ケ		
	ケ	ケ	ケ	ケ	ケ	ケ

re	レ	↓レ↗				
	レ	レ	レ	レ	レ	レ

ru	ル	⁾↓	ル↗			
	ル	ル	ル	ル	ル	ル

n	ン	↘	ン↗			
	ン	ン	ン	ン	ン	ン

shi	シ	↘	⸍↘	シ↗		
	シ	シ	シ	シ	シ	シ

ro	ロ	丨	ㄇ	ロ		
	ロ	ロ	ロ	ロ	ロ	ロ
o	ヲ	一	二	ヲ		
	ヲ	ヲ	ヲ	ヲ	ヲ	ヲ
e	エ	一	丁	エ		
	エ	エ	エ	エ	エ	エ
mo	モ	一	二	モ		
	モ	モ	モ	モ	モ	モ

su	ス	ス	ス			
	ス	ス	ス	ス	ス	ス

se	セ	セ	セ			
	セ	セ	セ	セ	セ	セ

nu	ヌ	ヌ	ヌ			
	ヌ	ヌ	ヌ	ヌ	ヌ	ヌ

ne	ネ	ネ	ネ	ネ	ネ	
	ネ	ネ	ネ	ネ	ネ	ネ

ki	キ	＝	＝	キ		
	キ	キ	キ	キ	キ	キ
ya	ヤ	⌐	ヤ			
	ヤ	ヤ	ヤ	ヤ	ヤ	ヤ
to	ト	｜	ト			
	ト	ト	ト	ト	ト	ト
o	オ	＝	ナ	オ		
	オ	オ	オ	オ	オ	オ

hi	ヒ	→⌐	↓ヒ→			
	ヒ	ヒ	ヒ	ヒ	ヒ	ヒ

ho	朩	→ㄧ	寸	↓寸→	朩	
	朩	朩	朩	朩	朩	朩

Exercises for Writing *Hiragana* and *Katakana* Words

Look at each sample in the upper square and write the same *kana* in the lower square.

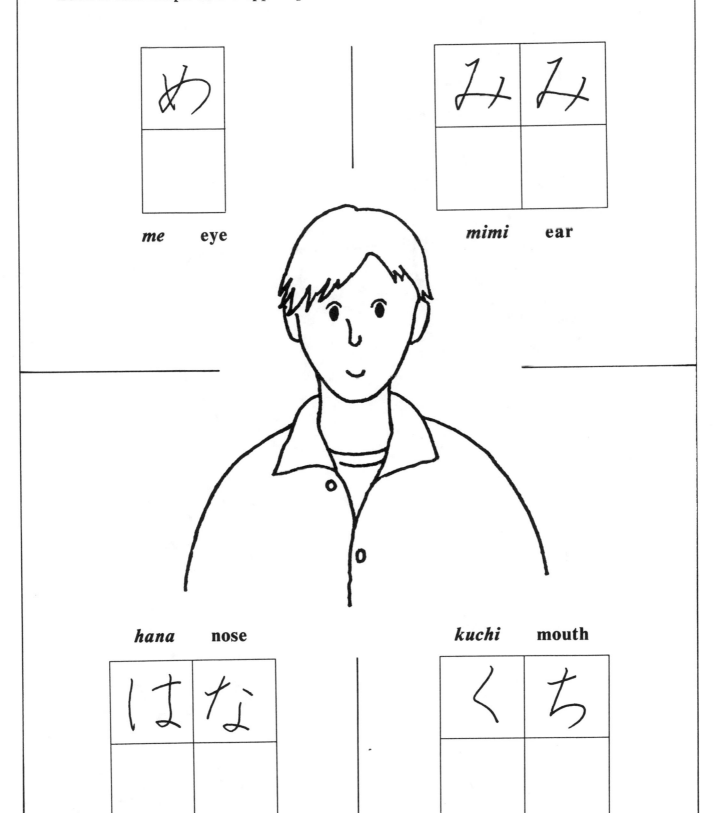

め

me   eye

みみ

mimi   ear

hana   nose

はな

kuchi   mouth

くち

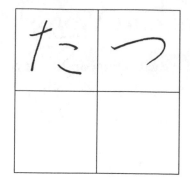

tatsu   to stand

suwaru   to sit

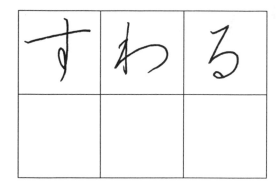

akeru   **to open**

あ	け	る

shimeru   **to shut**

し	め	る

hanasu   **to talk**

は	な	す

warau   **to laugh**

わ	ら	う

yomu   to read

よ　む

utau   to sing

う　た　う

hashiru   to run

は　し　る

arau   to wash

あ　ら　う

uru   to sell

う	る

kau   to buy

か	う

nomu   to drink

の	む

naku   to cry

な	く

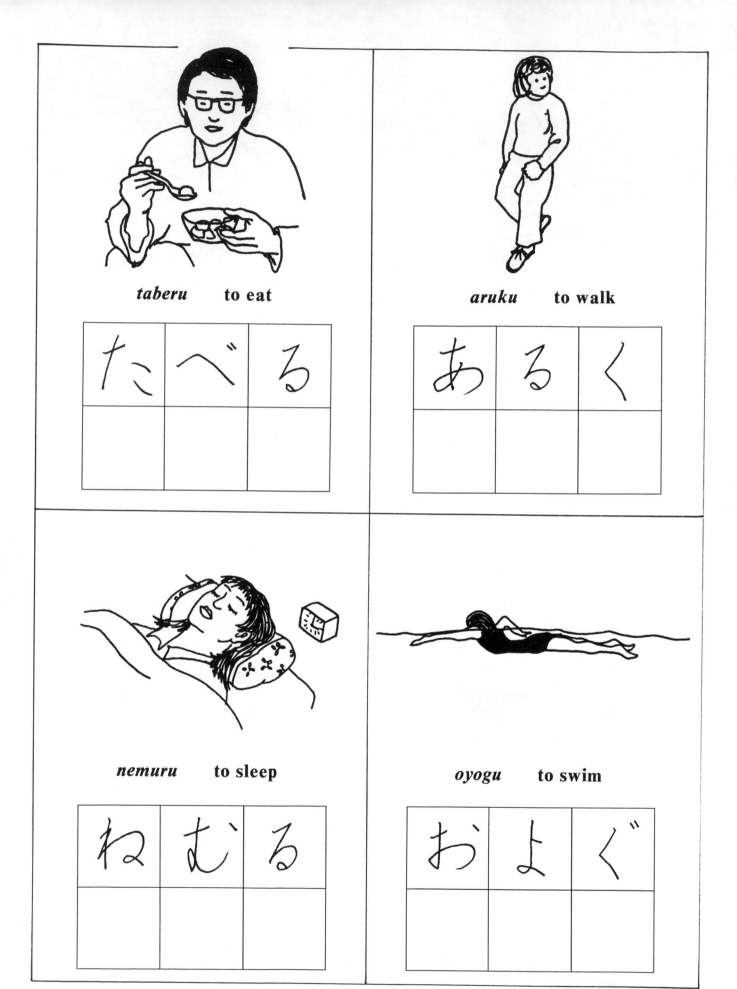

taberu   to eat

たべる

aruku   to walk

あるく

nemuru   to sleep

ねむる

oyogu   to swim

およぐ

risu   squirrel

tokage   lizard

り　す

と　か　げ

tora   tiger

kaeru   frog

と　ら

か　え　る

47

megane　　eyeglasses

めがね

enogu　　paints

えのぐ

taiko　　drum

たいこ

hōki　　broom

ほうき

hebi   snake

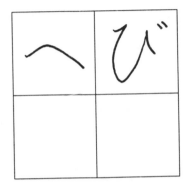

へび

bōshi   hat

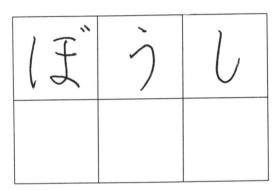

ぼうし

kaban   bag

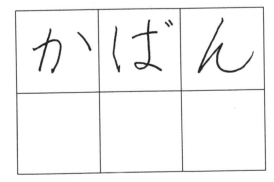

かばん

tai   sea bream

たい

kumo   spider

くも

ari   ant

あり

tanuki raccoon dog

たぬき

sakana   fish

さかな

uma   horse

う　ま

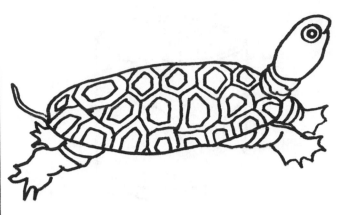

kame   turtle

か　め

chō   butterfly

ち　ょ　う

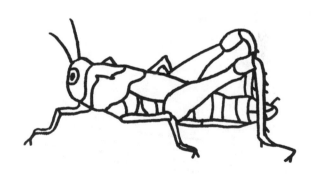

inago   locust

い　な　ご

yunomi   teacup

ゆ	の	み

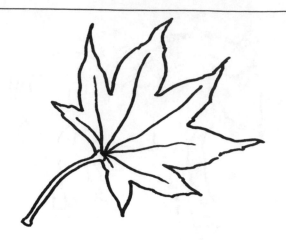

momiji   maple

も	み	じ

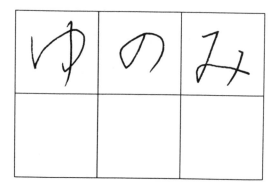

empitsu   pencil

え	ん	ぴ	つ

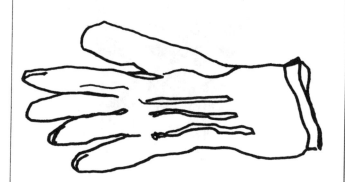

tebukuro   glove(s)

て	ぶ	く	ろ

kagami mirror

か	が	み

kabin vase

か	び	ん

tsukue desk

つ	く	え

denwa telephone

で	ん	わ

kuri   chestnut

くり

kame   jar

かめ

endō   peas

えんどう

takenoko bamboo sprout

たけのこ

inu　　**dog**

い　ぬ

neko　　cat

ね　こ

suzume　**sparrows**

す　ず　め

hitsuji　　**sheep**

ひ　つ　じ

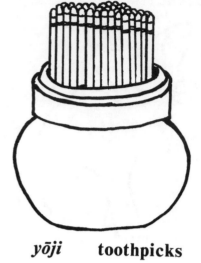

yōji   **toothpicks**

よ	う	じ

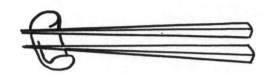

hashi   **chopsticks**

は	し

kutsu   **shoes**

く	つ

tokei   **clock**

と	け	い

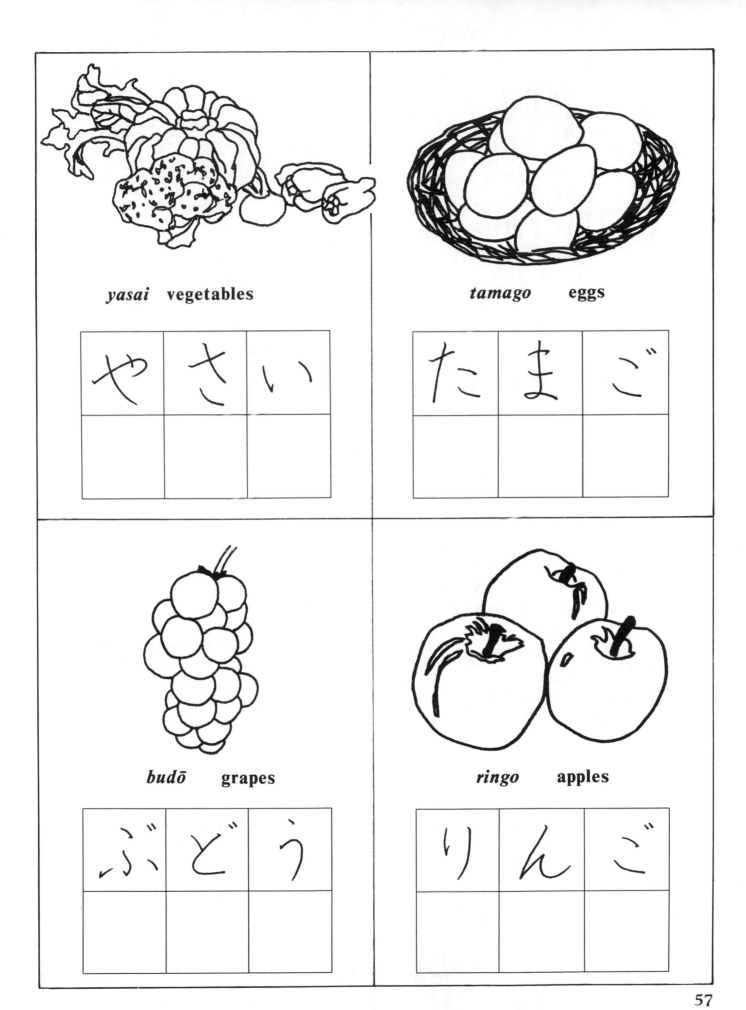

yasai   **vegetables**

やさい

tamago   **eggs**

たまご

budō   **grapes**

ぶどう

ringo   **apples**

りんご

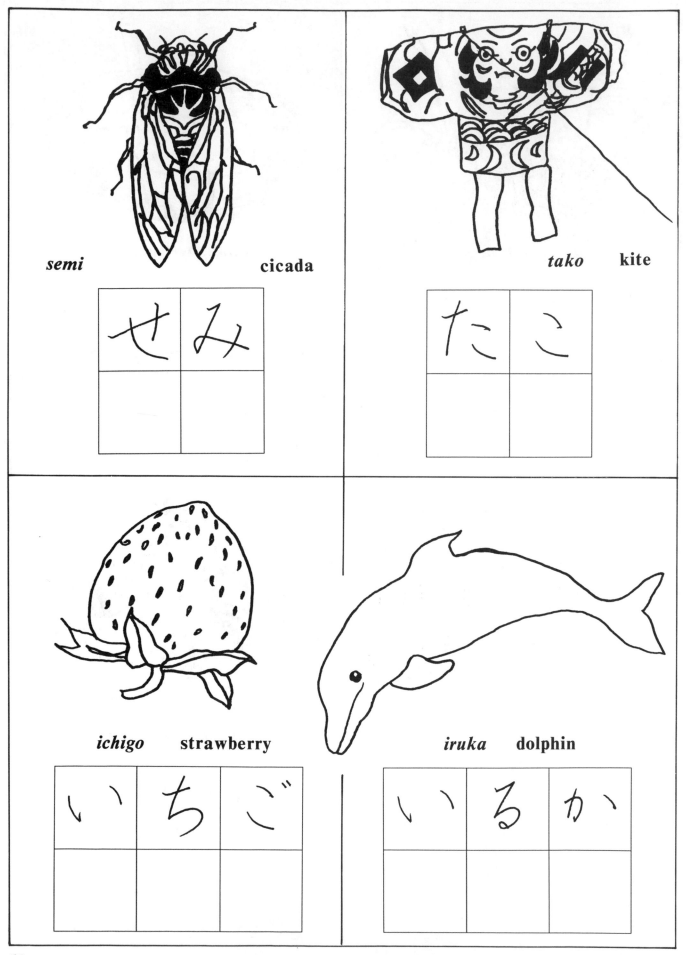

semi cicada

せみ

tako kite

たこ

ichigo strawberry

いちご

iruka dolphin

いるか

58

hake   brush

は け

fude   writing brush

ふ で

hasami   scissors

は さ み

ukiwa   water ring

う き わ

kagi   key

か　ぎ

kasa   umbrella

か　さ

tsumekiri   nail clipper

つ　め　き　り

sen'nuki   bottle opener

せ　ん　ぬ　き

suika   watermelon

す	い	か

imo   (sweet) potato

い	も

kai   shellfish

か	い

gohan   boiled rice

ご	は	ん

kirin　giraffe

き	り	ん

rakuda　camel

ら	く	だ

tsubame　swallow(s)

つ	ば	め

karasu　crow

か	ら	す

washi   eagle

わ	し

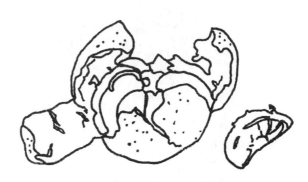

mikan   orange

み	か	ん

usagi   rabbit

う	さ	ぎ

bara   rose

ば	ら

yuku   **to go**

ゆ	く

kuru   **to come**

く	る

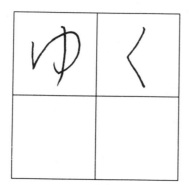

sakura   **cherry blossom**

さ	く	ら

suisen   **daffodil**

す	い	せ	ん

hane　　**feather**

は	ね

nasu　　**eggplant**

な	す

kudamono　　**fruit(s)**

く	だ	も	の

ajisai　　**hydrangea**

あ	じ	さ	い

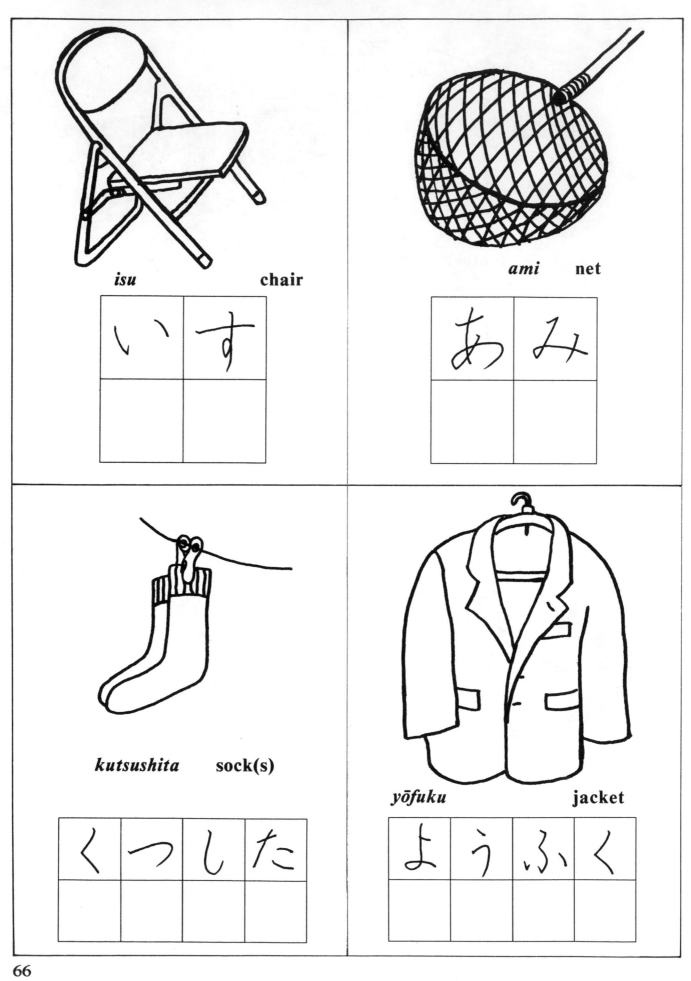

isu　　　chair

いす

ami　net

あみ

kutsushita　　sock(s)

くつした

yōfuku　　　jacket

ようふく

nashi　　pear

な	し

sensu　　fan

せ	ん	す

kaminari　thunder

か	み	な	り

haizara　　ashtray

は	い	ざ	ら

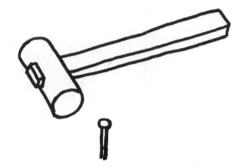

kanazuchi hammer

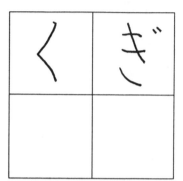

kugi nail

か	な	づ	ち

く	ぎ

kyūsu small teapot

nagagutsu boots

き	ゆ	う	す

な	が	ぐ	つ

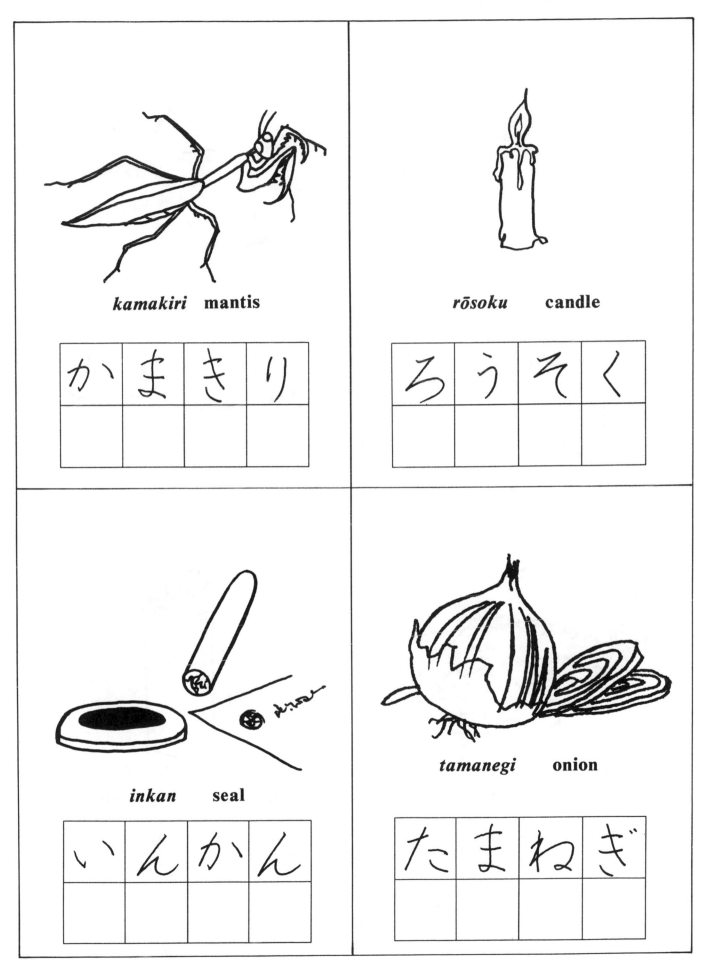

kamakiri   mantis

か	ま	き	り

rōsoku   candle

ろ	う	そ	く

inkan   seal

い	ん	か	ん

tamanegi   onion

た	ま	ね	ぎ

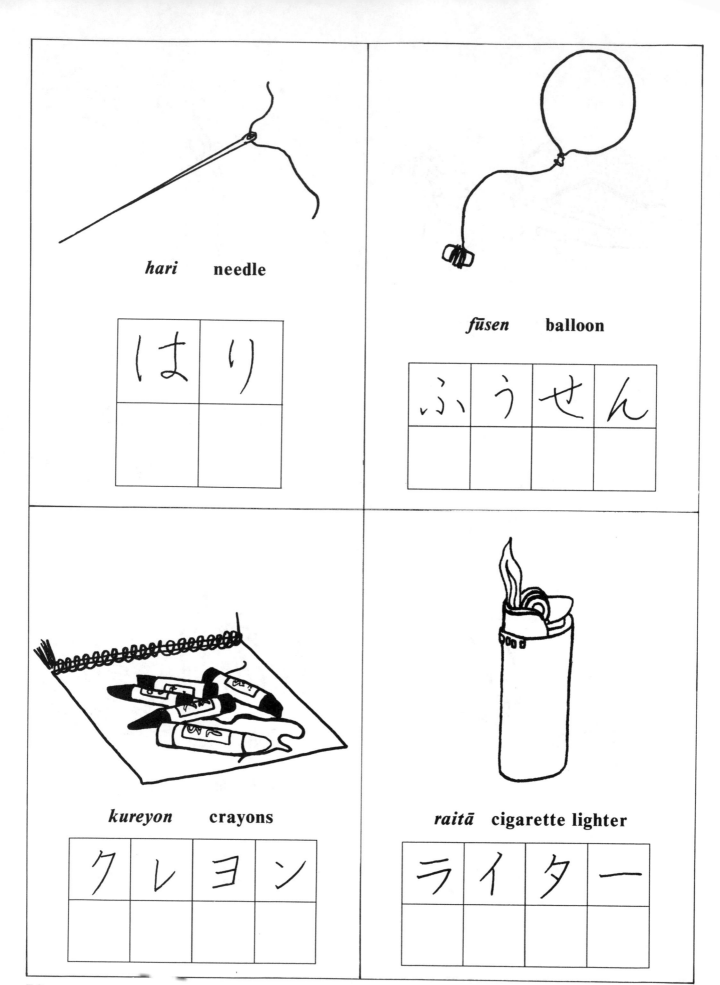

hari   needle

はり

fūsen   balloon

ふうせん

kureyon   crayons

クレヨン

raitā   cigarette lighter

ライター

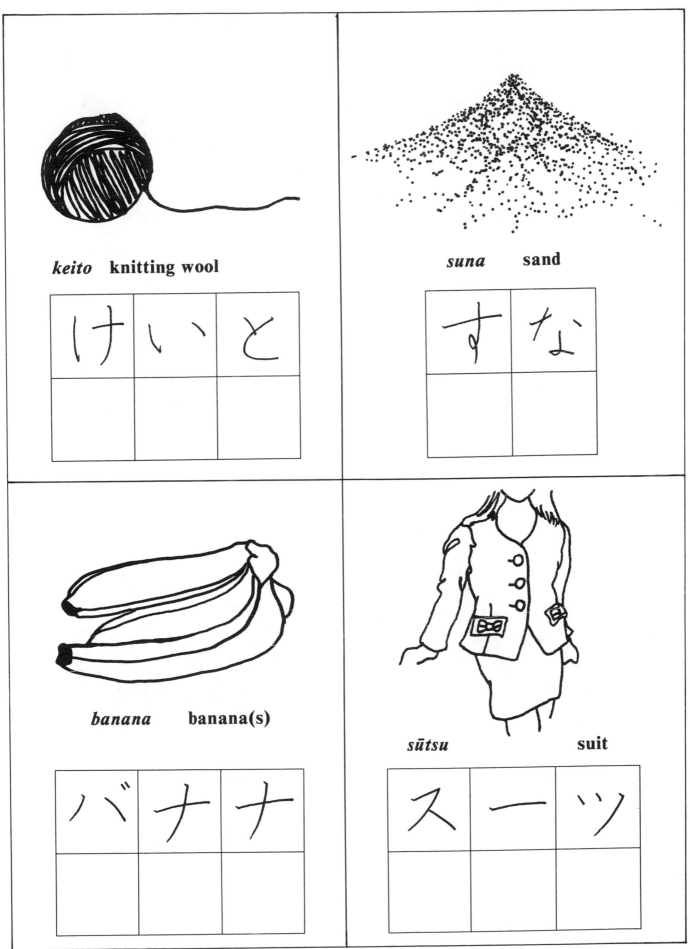

keito   knitting wool

けいと

suna   sand

すな

banana   banana(s)

バナナ

sūtsu   suit

スーツ

71

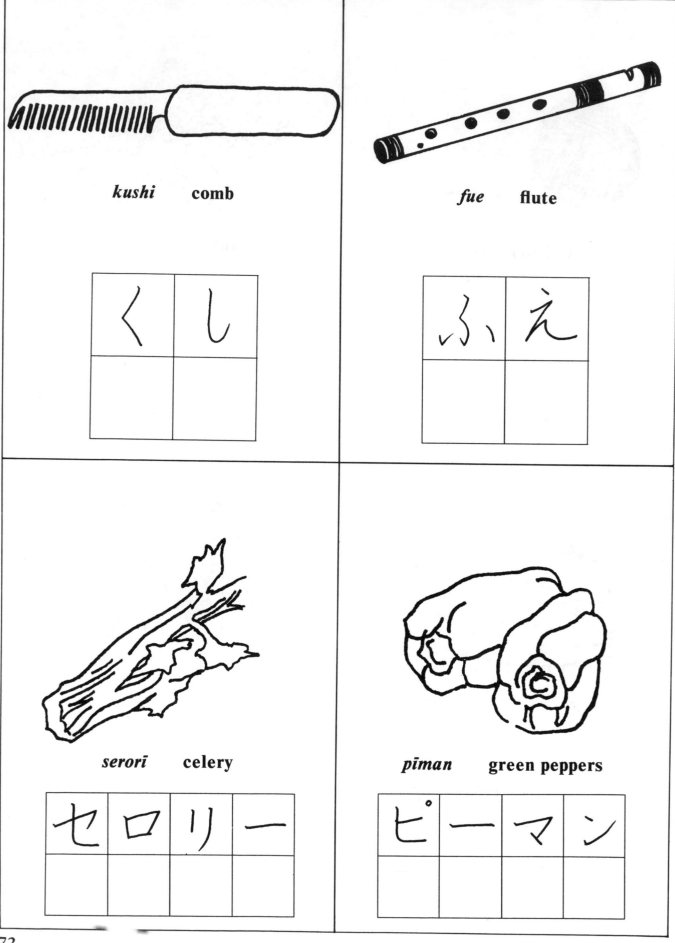

kushi   comb

くし

fue   flute

ふえ

serori   celery

セロリー

pīman   green peppers

ピーマン

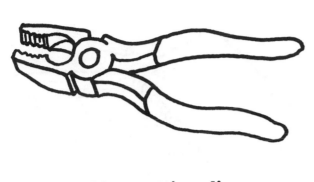

penchi   cutting pliers

ペ	ン	チ

kēki   cake

ケ	ー	キ

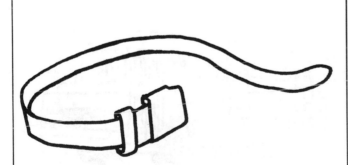

beruto   belt

ベ	ル	ト

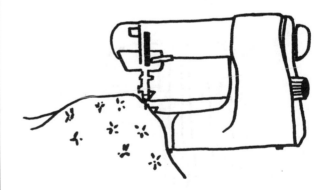

mishin   sewing machine

ミ	シ	ン

pen　　pen

ペン

nōto　　notebook

ノート

taoru　　towel

タオル

basu　　bus

バス

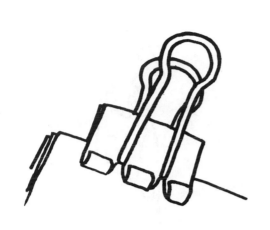

kurippu　　**paper clip**

ク	リ	ッ	プ

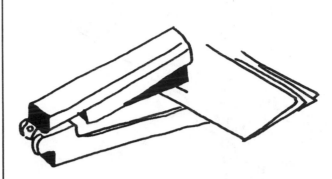

hochikisu　**stapler**

ホ	チ	キ	ス

kattā　　**cutter**

カ	ッ	タ	ー

sutando　**table lamp**

ス	タ	ン	ド

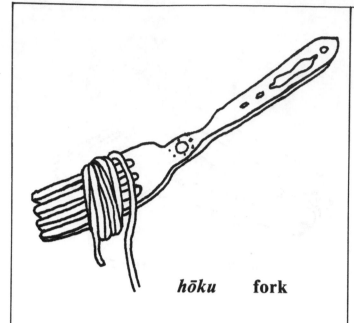

hōku   **fork**

フ	ォ	ー	ク

nekutai   **necktie**

ネ	ク	タ	イ

kakuteru **cocktail**

カ	ク	テ	ル

pengin   **penguin**

ペ	ン	ギ	ン

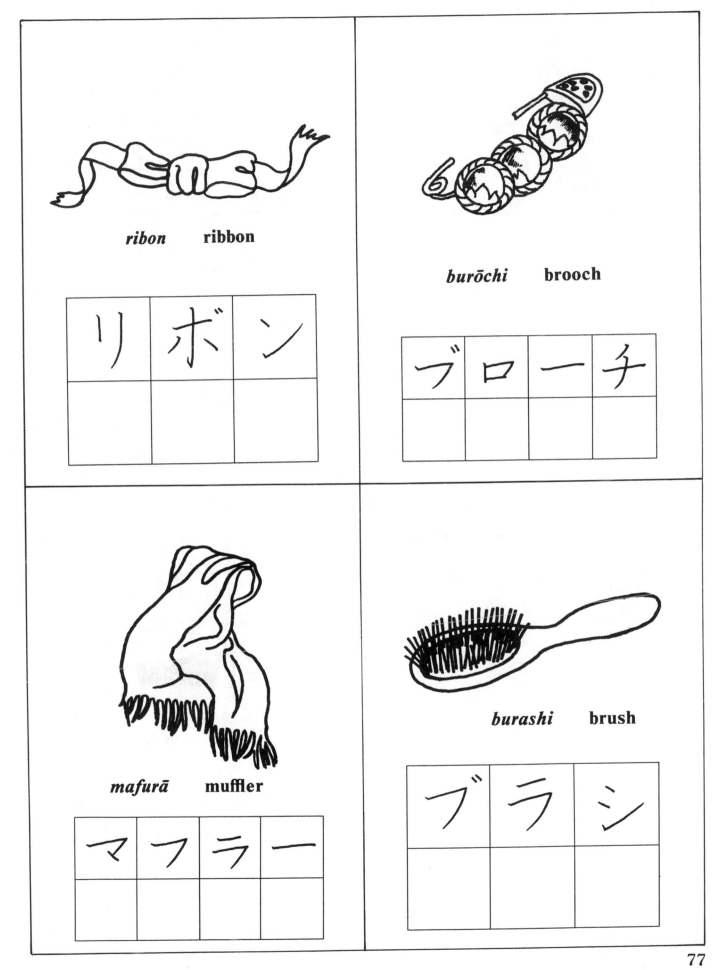

ribon   ribbon

リ | ボ | ン

burōchi   brooch

ブ | ロ | ー | チ

mafurā   muffler

マ | フ | ラ | ー

burashi   brush

ブ | ラ | シ

Pari   Paris

Rōma   Rome

Pekin   Beijing

botan   button

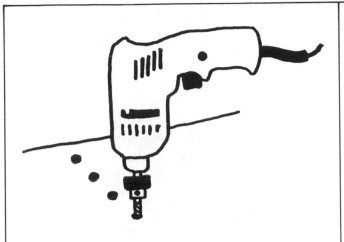

doriru   electric drill

ド	リ	ル

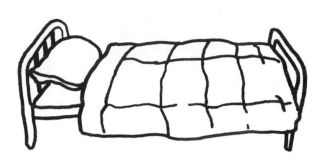

beddo   bed

ベ	ッ	ド

jīnzu   jeans

ジ	ー	ン	ズ

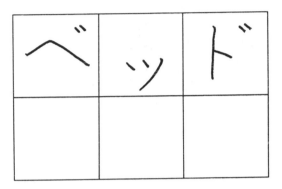

airon   iron

ア	イ	ロ	ン

potto　　thermos

ポ	ッ	ト

kōhī　　coffee

コ	ー	ヒ	ー

supūn　　spoon

ス	プ	ー	ン

purin　　pudding

プ	リ	ン

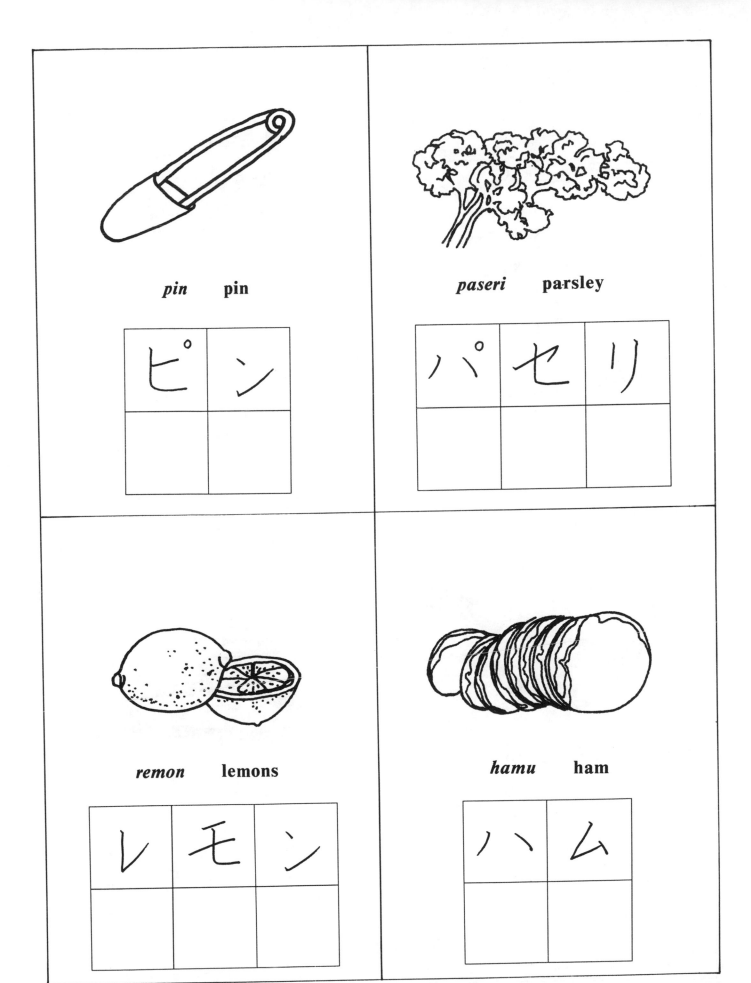

pin　pin

ピ	ン

paseri　par-sley

パ	セ	リ

remon　lemons

レ	モ	ン

hamu　ham

ハ	ム

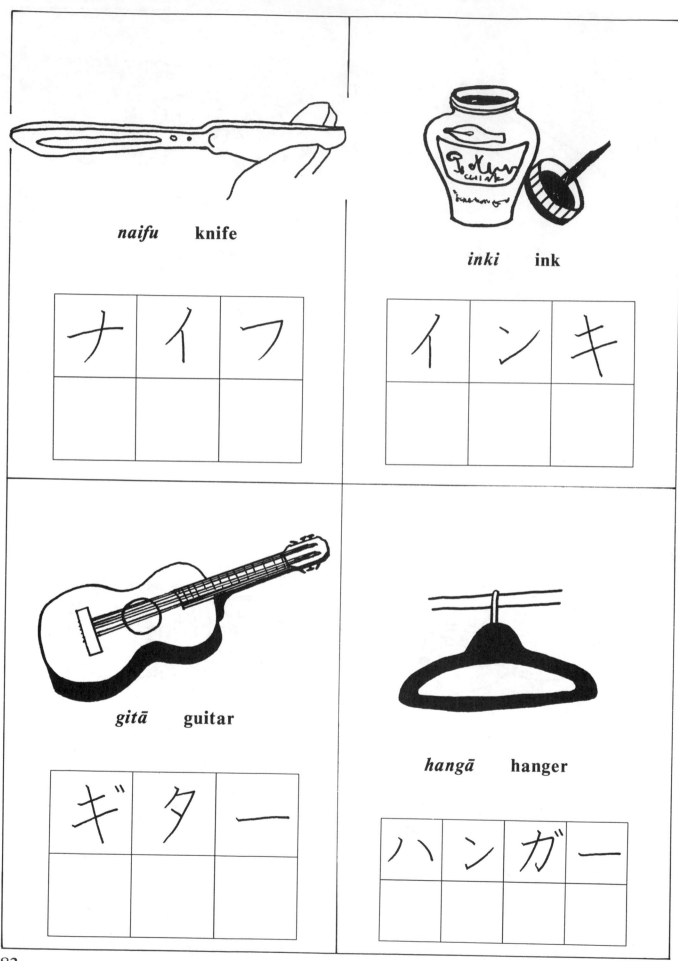

naifu　knife

inki　ink

ナ　イ　フ

イ　ン　キ

gitā　guitar

hangā　hanger

ギ　タ　ー

ハ　ン　ガ　ー

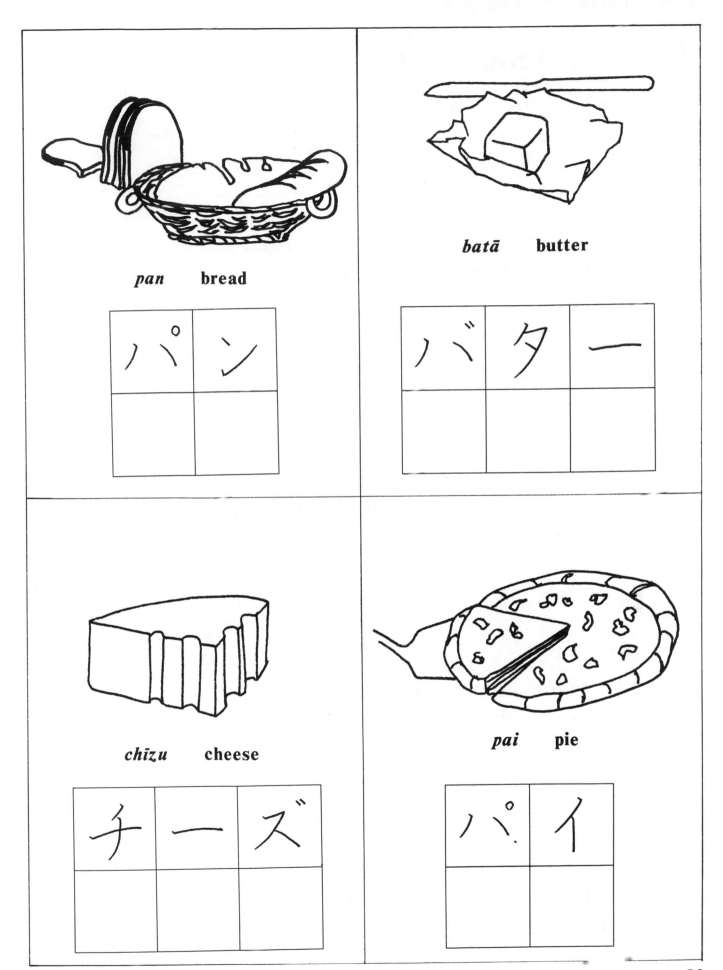

pan   bread

パン

batā   butter

バター

chīzu   cheese

チーズ

pai   pie

パイ

Short Sentences with Kana

Trace over the dotted lines and complete each sentence.

Watashi wa asa roku-ji ni okimasu.
I wake up at six in the morning.

Otōsan wa basu de kaisha ni ikimasu.
My father goes to (his) company by bus.

Gakkō made san-kiro arimasu.
It is three kilometers to the school.

Okāsan wa ryōri ga jōzu desu.
My mother is a good cook.

きのうともだちと、ピクニック
にいきました。

Kinō tomodachi to pikunikku ni ikimashita.
Yesterday I went on a picnic with friends.

ちょうちょうがにひき、はなに
とまっています。

Chōchō ga ni-hiki hana ni tomatte imasu.
Two butterflies are stopping at a flower.

ジュースをのみますか、コーラ
にしますか。

Jūsu o nomimasu ka, kōra ni shimasu ka?
Would you like (some) juice or cola?

できれば、コーヒーをおねがい
します。

Dekireba kōhī o onegai shimasu.
If I could, I'd like to have coffee.

| | デ | パ | ー | ト | で | 、 | ぼ | う | し | を | か | い | ま | し |
| | た | 。 | | | | | | | | | | | | |

Depāto de bōshi o kaimashita.
I bought a hat at a department store.

| | あ | の | ひ | と | は | 、 | ス | キ | ー | の | せ | ん | し | ゅ |
| | で | す | 。 | | | | | | | | | | | |

Ano hito wa sukī no senshu desu.
That person (over there) is a skier.

| | い | ぬ | と | ね | こ | は | 、 | ど | ち | ら | が | す | き | で |
| | す | か | 。 | | | | | | | | | | | |

Inu to neko wa dochira ga suki desu ka?
Which do you prefer, dogs or cats?

| | ら | い | ね | ん | の | カ | レ | ン | ダ | ー | を | さ | し | あ |
| | げ | ま | す | 。 | | | | | | | | | | |

Rainen no karendā o sashiagemasu.
I will give you next year's calendar.

*Watashi-tachi wa dōbutsuen no iriguchi de kippu o
kaimashita.*

We bought tickets at the entrance to the zoo.

Kyōshitsu de hashitte wa ikemasen.
You should not run in the classroom.

Minasan, shizuka ni shimashō.
Let's be quiet, everyone.

Tēburu no ue ni painappuru ga itsutsu arimasu.
Five pineapples are on the table.

Dizunīrando made aruite dore kurai kakarimasu ka?
How long does it take to walk to Disneyland?

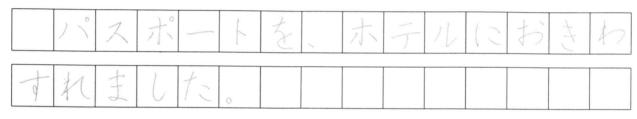

Pasupōto o hoteru ni oki-wasuremashita.
I forgot my passport at the hotel.

Ano hito-tachi wa sakkā no shiai o terebi de mite imasu.
Those people are watching a soccer match on television.

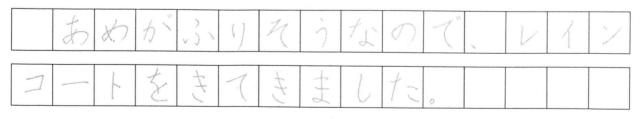

Ame ga furi sō nanode reinkōto o kite kimashita.
It looks as though it's going to rain, so I wore a raincoat.

Erebētā de okujō ni agarimashō.
Let's take the elevator to the roof.

*Mukashi, mukashi arutokoro ni ojī-san to obā-san ga
sunde imashita.*
Long, long ago there lived an old man and an old woman.

Watashi-tachi wa, natsu niwa pūru de oyogimasu.
We swim in the pool in summer.

よくてをあらいなさい。

Yoku te o arai nasai.
Wash your hands well.

Onīsan wa, wain yori uisukī no hō ga suki desu.
My older brother likes whiskey better than wine.

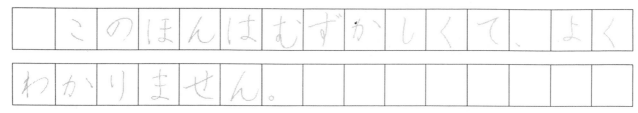

Kono hon wa muzukashikute yoku wakarimasen.
This book is difficult, and I don't understand it.

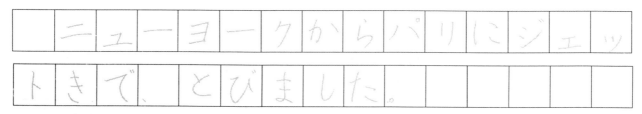

Nyūyōku kara Parī ni jetto-ki de tobimashita.
I flew from New York to Paris in a jet airplane.

Yōroppa dewa Mirano to Uīn ni itta ko to ga arimasu.
In Europe, I have been to Milan and Vienna.

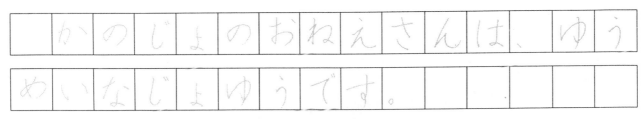

かれからクリスマス・カードをうけとりました。

Kare kara kurisumasu kādo o uketormashita.
I received a Christmas card from him.

かのじょのおねえさんは、ゆうめいなじょゆうです。

Kanojo no onēsan wa yūmei na joyū desu.
Her older sister is a famous actress.

おとうといもうとは、ふゆになるとスケートをしてあそびます。

Otōto to imōto wa, fuyu ni naru to sukēto o shite asobimasu.
When winter comes, my younger brother and sister enjoy skating.

Exercise Sheet Date: Name:

Copy these 5 pages to use as exercise sheets.

Date: Name: **Exercise Sheet**

Exercise Sheet

Date: Name:

Date: Name: **Exercise Sheet**